When You Wonder

"Why?"

by
R. W. SCHAMBACH

POWER PUBLICATIONS • TYLER, TEXAS

Other Books in the
R. W. Schambach *Legacy Series*

When You Wonder "Why?"

Power of Faith for Today's Christian

Triumphant Faith

Power Struggle *Faith for Difficult Relationships*

Contents

INTRODUCTION

And it came to pass, when Pharaoh had let the people go, that God led them not through the way of the land of the Philistines, although that was near; for God said, Lest peradventure the people repent when they see war, and they return to Egypt: But God led the people about, through the way of the wilderness of the Red sea: and the children of Israel went up harnessed out of the land of Egypt. And Moses took the bones of Joseph with him: for he had straitly sworn the children of Israel, saying, God will surely visit you; and ye shall carry up my bones away hence with you.

And they took their journey from Succoth, and encamped in Etham, in the edge of the wilderness. And the Lord went before them by day in a pillar of a cloud, to lead them the way; and by night in a pillar of fire, to give them light; to go by day and night: He took not away the pillar of the cloud by day, nor the pillar of fire by night, from before the people.

— Exodus 13:17-22

Chapter 1

The Discipline of the Winding Path

But God led the people about...And the Lord went before them by day in a pillar of a cloud, to lead them the way; and by night in a pillar of fire, to give them light; to go by day and night (Exodus 13:18,21).

The ability to be led by the Spirit of God often brings God's children to a place of discipline. Nobody enjoys being disciplined. I don't care who you are — if you *want* discipline, something is wrong with your thinking! But God disciplines us for our own good. We don't *want* the discipline. And sometimes we don't *like* it. But that doesn't stop God from doing it. He knows we need it.

Verse 18 says, *the children of Israel went up harnessed.* Another translation says they went up *disciplined* out of the land of Egypt.

Do you ever wonder why it seems that God always does things the hard way? The Bible says He did not take them through the way of the land of the Philistines, although that was closer. There's always a way that seems easier. We're always looking for a shortcut, an easy way out. And when it comes to the spiritual life, many times God puts us or allows us to get into situations that discipline us. And He doesn't discipline us our way, it's got to come God's way.

Everybody's looking for what I call a "Burger King" religion — "Have it your way!" People want their own kind of religion. But you can't have it your way. You've got to have it God's way or you're not going to have it at all. God will bring you to a winding path to discipline you.

When I was just a 17-year-old lad, I joined the United States Navy. World War II was still going on and I just knew if I could get into the service, I could bring that war to a close. There's nobody's ego like your own ego, isn't that right? So I went down and joined the Navy.

The recruiting officer really courted me. He took me out to eat...treated me so nice...smiled at me all the time. And as long as he was courting me, everything was fine. I was a prospect for the Navy.

But just as soon as I signed my name on the dotted line, a metamorphosis set in and that man's character changed in a split moment of time. As soon as I signed the papers, he yelled, "All right, sailor. Attention!"

He caught me by surprise but I yelled right back. "Hey, buddy, wait a minute..."

"Don't 'buddy' me. Shut up!" he said. You're not your own anymore. You don't belong to your mama now. You belong to the United States Navy. We just bought you for $50 a month. From now on, you go to bed when we tell you to go to bed. You get up when we tell you to get up. You eat when we say eat. And when we say run, you run. We're going to discipline you, boy. We're going to make a sailor out of you."

I stood there with my jaw dropped all the way down to the floor. All I could think was, *"And I wanted to board a warship and have the Navy send me to the Pacific to whip the Japanese into shape!"* But the first thing they did was put me in a boot camp. Discipline. It was no longer me giving orders but the commanding officer giving orders.

God Wants to Discipline You

Listen to me, saints. It's the same way when you get saved. You didn't choose God, God chose you. He called you, ordained you. And He is trying to discipline you to the place where He can lead you, guide you, and direct you by His Spirit.

You may not like this, but I'm going to preach it anyhow. Some people are looking for a preacher or a church to tell them what to do. They're looking for an evangelist to follow. I know some people that followed an evangelist down to Guyana and they're dead now! If you are going to follow somebody, you'd better follow Jesus. He's the One Who called you. He's the One Who guides. And He will lead you and guide you into *all* truth.

You may not want to follow the winding path, but when God says go, you'd better go. You'd better submit to Him.

We don't have a visible cloud and a visible fire to follow today. But we've got the Holy Ghost living inside of us. And He'll lead us and guide us.

Discipline Helps You Defeat the Devil

In Exodus 13:17, God said He didn't take the children of Israel out the easy way, the way that was near. He said, *Lest peradventure the people repent when they see war, and they return to Egypt...*

This Christian life we've been called to is no Sunday school picnic. This is war! We are in a conflict. This is no barbecue supper or fried-chicken meeting. We are engaged in a battle.

The world out there hates God's people. Yet here we are trying to be friends with the world. The world despises you. The world out there is controlled by an enemy, and that enemy is the devil.

Do you know why the devil hates you? Because when you got saved, he lost a soul he thought he had. He thought you were going to Hell with him.

But God detoured your way and saved you — reached down in the midst of sin, picked you up, washed you in His blood, put a robe of righteousness on you, and recorded your name in the Lamb's Book of Life. And now He calls you "Son." No wonder the devil is mad.

But the Church has lost its ability to confront the devil and we've been running from the enemy. God never intended for you to run from the devil. He's given you the equipment for your head, your chest, your loins, your feet. You've got a sword in one hand and a shield in the other hand. *But there is no protection for your back.* Why? Because God never intended for you and me to run from the devil. God said one of you shall chase a thousand and two of you will put 10,000 to flight. According to those odds, three believers can move 100,000 and four of us can defeat a million.

We need to quit running from the devil. If anybody needs to run, it's the devil! And we're going to run after him just to let him know that *greater is he that is in [us], than he that is in the world* (I John 4:4).

The children of Israel were enslaved to the people of Egypt. But God saved them and brought them out of bondage. So they went out, got their first taste of war, and said, "Huh uh, let's go back to the onions and the garlics. Lord, at least in Egypt we had three meals a day. And we didn't have to fight!"

Some folks like bondage. I don't! I was set free. And He whom the Son sets free is free indeed (see John 8:36). Thank God, I'm free at last!

At one time or another, everyone gets into a

situation where he wonders why. I had a lady tell me not long ago, "Brother Schambach, how come I got to go through all this Hell? I'm living the best I know how. My next door neighbor is a numbers writer and the neighbor on the other side plays the lottery. There's a gambler down the street. They ain't never got no trouble."

I said, "Why should they have trouble? They're going to Hell anyway. You're the one the devil is after. He's not going to mess with his own."

Sometimes God allows us to get into a troublesome situation so that He can do battle with the devil. Always remember that it isn't your fight — the battle is the Lord's. And He will use you to defeat the enemy and let you enjoy the victory. But notice this — God has given you weapons for warfare. The Holy Ghost is your Strengthener and gives you God's marching orders for battle. God's given you His Word as your shield and His blood for protection. And above all else you have the name of Jesus to stop every attack of the enemy.

But these weapons won't do you any good unless you're in a situation to use them. God may allow you to get in a predicament so you'll learn how to use your weapons. Your weapons are not carnal (fleshly), but mighty through God (see 2 Corinthians 10:4). And He assures you victory through Jesus!

Every time you meet the devil head-on, pick up your weapons and defeat him. Put him under your feet where he belongs! Don't be afraid of war as the children of Israel were. You already have the victory!

When you realize this, you've got it made. If

God is the One who called you to victory — and He did — He'll make sure you win every time if you'll be obedient to His leading. That's all He wants. In fact, He demands obedience. God told the children of Israel as He brought them out of bondage, "I'm going to give you a visible sign — a cloud by day and a pillar of fire by night. When the cloud moves, you move. When the fire moves, you move. When the cloud stops, you stop, or you are on your own."

Somebody says, "I wish I had that cloud today."

You've got it. It's the Holy Ghost. Some folks deny themselves that Guide. The Holy Ghost is more than a tongue. The Holy Ghost is a Person. And He will lead you and guide you. He'll help you come against every enemy and put the devil where he belongs.

The enemy has no business attacking your son or daughter. The devil has no business on your back. He has no business hurting your body or squeezing your pocketbook. There's only one place that enemy has any right to be — under your feet in the place of defeat! Hallelujah!

Thank God, He's still on the throne. He's got everything under control. It's not my battle, but it's His battle. He's the One who called me. And He's the One who will see me through. *He which hath begun a good work in you will perform it until the day of Jesus Christ* (Philippians 1:6).

Discipline Makes You Depend on God

Most of us try to find the easy way out. And we miss one of the greatest blessings. God's trying to put us into a place where we are solely dependent on Him. Many times He will allow you to get into a situation where there ain't nothing you can do but trust Him. But your way out is already assured. God already has it planned.

God told Moses to move the people down to the Red Sea. Now the sea was overflowing its banks, mountains on either side. It looked like there was no way out.

And sure enough, here comes the army of Pharaoh. Pharaoh laughs and says, "I've got them. There's no way out!" Maybe the devil has been laughing at you, saying, "There's no way out. Your back is against the wall."

Somebody says, "I'm down to my last $10."

You blew it. You should have put it in the offering and got down to nothing. When you get to nothing, God's *got* to perform a miracle!

Someone else says, "My doctor gave up on me." It's about time! Now the Great Physician can work on you.

You say, "I'm at the end of my rope." Then tie a knot in it and hang on. Help is on the way. God's got your miracle for you. The way out is assured. Now when the devil gets close, when you can feel his breath coming down on your neck, don't be tempted to do battle your way.

Look at Exodus 14:10, *And when Pharaoh*

drew nigh, [Pharaoh is a type of the devil] *the children of Israel lifted up their eyes, and, behold, the Egyptians marched after them; and they were sore afraid.* The human response is to be fearful when trouble comes. I don't care who you are, when you find that devil breathing down your neck, fear grips your heart. But you don't have to be afraid. When you see the enemy coming after you, pick up your weapons and fight.

This foul devil, the thief, comes to kill, to steal, and to destroy (see John 10:10). The devil despises you, hates you. He's out to kill your children. That's why we have so many women being deceived into aborting their babies today because the devil kills.

I had a lady come to me one time and say, "Brother Schambach, I've been in the church 30 years and the devil has never bothered me. But I came to your meeting last week and got saved, and I've been going through Hell ever since."

Notice what she said — been in the church and the devil never bothered her. But you get born again and begin to serve God and He will spew out every kind of foul devil on your front doorstep. The devil will be all over your case trying to drag you back into the mess God delivered you from. *When the enemy shall come in like a flood, the spirit of the Lord shall lift up a standard against him* (see Isaiah 59:19).

Tell the devil, "Greater is He that is in me than he that is in the world."

Jesus gave you power over all the powers of

the devil. In His name, you shall cast out devils. Did Jesus say that? Then your way out is assured. Now listen, if the devil is on your trail, that's a sure sign you've got something. That ought to make you shout a little bit. What's the devil bothering with you for? Did he ever bother with you when you were serving him? You never even knew he was around. And you thought you were religious.

Remember when you first got saved? Here comes the devil sneaking around, saying, "You're not saved." Did he ever come and say you weren't saved before? Well, how come he is doing it now? Because he is a LIAR.

Oh, come on, devil, tell me some more lies.

"You're not healed."

Thank you, devil. Thank you for telling me I'm not healed. That must mean I AM healed because you are a liar. You know what my Bible says? *Many are the afflictions of the righteous:* *BUT the Lord delivereth him out of them ALL* (Psalm 34:19, emphasis mine). Hallelujah!

The devil is a liar. Don't give up. Hang in there. Victory is coming your way. This is the way out of bondage.

Discipline Requires Participation

When I was a sinner, I liked to fight. Since I got saved, I *still* like to fight. And there's one fight I know I'm going to win every time — the fight against the devil.

God has assured your way out. So long as you know you're going to win the fight, don't worry about fighting. You are the victor and not the victim. You are the conqueror, not the conquered. You are the overcomer and not the one that's overcome. God never intended for His kids to be overcome by the devil. So our way out of this mess is assured.

But God demands participation. He told Moses to tell the children of Israel to go forward (see Exodus 14:15). That was their part. God said to Moses, "Say to the people — participate."

And Moses said, *"Fear ye not, stand still, and see the salvation of the Lord"* (Exodus 14:13). God allows us to get into certain situations so we can be still and see Him at work.

Moses told the Israelites, "You will not see this enemy after today. So don't be afraid anymore — stand still. The battle is not your battle, but God's battle."

Then God orders Moses — here comes the participation now — "Tell My people to go forward."

I can just picture Moses looking up to Heaven and muttering, "Forward? But the sea, Lord." Moses was on his knees crying and praying, almost in unbelief.

God interrupted him and said, "Would you get off your knees! You're wasting time. Don't you know Pharaoh's on your case?"

I believe in prayer, but there comes a time when you have to quit praying and start believing — start putting legs on those prayers. That's what God is telling His people today.

God always says, "Go forward. GO FORWARD!"

Faith can only go one way — forward. Faith doesn't back up. Faith doesn't detour. Moses said, "Lord, did you forget the sea?"

"What is that I put in your hand?" God asked.

"The rod," Moses answered.

"Well, use it!"

"The rod? Now, Lord, I know that rod can float, but it ain't going to float no three and a half million people!" We always wonder how God is going to get us out of this mess. You might as well stop wondering and worrying. You'll never be able to think of the solution because God's going to do it some supernatural way.

God said, "Moses, stretch out the rod." Here's the participation! Moses had to stretch out that rod in front of three and a half million people. And when he did, the waters backed up.

Now, get this — the Bible says it took them all night to cross the Red Sea. *All night.* Imagine how big a path God had to put in the Red Sea to get three and a half million across? My good friend, Rev. Bert Clendennen, put this problem on his computer, and you know what that computer came up with? In order for God to get three and a half million people across the Red Sea in one night, He had to cut a path through the Red Sea five miles wide!

God is a big God. And He's got a way out.

Perhaps you are involved in a courtroom situation right now, wondering *How am I going to get out of this thing?* God's got a way out.

Maybe you are holding the final decree — the divorce papers — in your hand. It looks like there's no way out. But I tell you there is a way out. God works in mysterious ways, His wonders to perform.

I don't care how financially embarrassed you are. Your back may be against the wall. The doctors may have turned you out. They may say your heart isn't beating right. I don't care if it beats only once a week — God will still heal you. God is a Miracle Worker.

God set a trap for the devil. When His people went over on the dry ground and got on the other side, they turned around and looked. Here comes Pharaoh. I can just picture Pharaoh on the other side with his horses and chariots. The captain of the squad gives orders to follow after the children of Israel. "If they can do it, we can do it!"

God's sitting in Heaven, saying, "Go ahead, Pharaoh."

So Pharaoh's whole army plunges across the path God cut out of the Red Sea. God waits till Pharaoh's army is in the right place. Then He says to Moses, "Take up the rod again, Moses. Stretch it back over the water. They're in the trap now." And the waters came back to their normal course and swallowed Pharaoh's army — horses, chariots, and every soldier.

On the other side, Miriam got ahold of her tambourine and said, "Come on, girls, get your dancing shoes out. The horse and the rider are thrown into the sea." God used Moses and the children of Israel to put the devil in the trap where he belonged.

God is looking for a people who will be disciplined, who will learn how to take orders from Him, and lead the devil into the trap. Then we will have the victory — every time!

A woman came into my meeting in Chicago back in the '60s with a piece of paper in her hand. It said, DISPOSSESSED. This woman walked down the center aisle of the church, weeping and crying. She said, "Oh, Brother Schambach, they are going to put me out on the street. I'm four months behind on my rent."

"The devil's a liar," I yelled. "He's not going to put God's children out on the sidewalk!"

"My mama is blind," she said, "and all I can see is my mama sitting out on the sidewalk. What am I going to do?"

I said, "You are going to hush."

"But what about the dispossess notice?"

I took it from her and tore it up. I threw it under the platform. "Forget it. You're looking at the wrong thing. God said He would supply all your needs according to His riches in glory by Christ Jesus. Now you sit right down here in the front."

"What am I going to do?" she asked.

And I replied, "You're going to hush and listen to me preach!"

"But the man's coming at 10:00 o'clock in the morning!" (This was Sunday night.) "Monday morning at 10:00, he's going to be there!"

I stood right in front of that woman and preached to her all night long. I preached everything I ever knew on faith to try to encourage her.

I didn't take the offering until I got done. I did that on purpose because she'd told me she tried to give the man $50 and he threw it back at her. He said he wanted it all, not just a piece of it. So I knew she had something to put in the offering. Maybe her landlord wouldn't take it, but I wanted her to give to God.

I said to her, "Now, it's time to receive the offering."

She looked at me and exclaimed, "Brother Schambach, don't you remember me? I *need* money!"

"I know it, girl. Where's your pocketbook? Now don't fight me. Ten o'clock Monday morning will be here soon. It's ten o'clock tonight, girl. You've got 12 hours. Go get your purse. Where is it?"

"Mama's got it," she answered. She was getting testy with me. In fact, she got downright mad at me. But I knew she was going to get glad again because in my spirit I knew what God was going to do.

She went back to where her blind mother was sitting. Then back she came. I held the bucket and turned my head. I knew she was mad, and I didn't know whether she was going to hit me with her purse or what. But she dropped something in the bucket. I didn't even know what it was until the next night.

After the offering was received, I said, "Get me your blind mother. I want to pray for her first. And you'll be number two in the line."

I'll never forget this as long as I live. I tell about this woman everywhere I go. I laid hands on that woman who had been blind for 20-some years. I commanded that blind spirit to turn loose of her — commanded sight to be restored! In my spirit I knew God healed her. But there was no evident sign of sight.

I asked the mother, "Will you do what I tell you to do?" She answered, "Anything you say, I'll do it."

"I want you to thank God for perfect vision until your head hits the pillow," I told her. "If you'll do what I tell you, you'll wake up seeing."

She said, "I'll do it." And off she went, down the ramp, usher on each side, saying, "Devil, you're a liar. I'm not blind no more. The man of God prayed. I'm healed. Lord, I thank You for perfect sight in Jesus' name."

Remember, she couldn't see. No sight! Anybody can thank God for sight when he can see. But it takes faith to thank Him when you don't have it.

Then I approached the daughter who'd gotten the dispossess notice and laid hands on her. I said, "Lord, I don't know how You're going to do this, but do it, in the name of Jesus." I said, "Go on home, woman. Unpack your bags, you're not going anywhere."

"How do you know I got bags packed?" she asked.

"The way you're talking I'm surprised you haven't moved yet!"

"Well, I did move half of it over to my brother's house."

"Go get it. You're not going anywhere," I told her.

On Monday night, the back door of the church burst open about 10 minutes after 8:00 p.m. Here comes this lady running down the center aisle, yelling "Whoopee! Glory!"

I stood up and said, "Stop, stop, stop, woman!"

"Brother Schambach, don't you remember me?"

"I remember you. But I want to ask you something. Why didn't you come to church like this last night?"

I gave her the microphone and said, "I can tell God did something for you." Then she proceeded to preach a message. I mean, she tore the place up that night. I didn't even have to preach.

She said, "It all happened this morning. I was awakened with the smell of bacon frying, coffee brewing, and homemade bread in the oven. I sat up in the bed and looked over at my blind mama's bed, and it was empty. I quickly threw on a robe and ran out into the kitchen. There was my blind mama making my breakfast for the first time in 20 years. I said, "Mama, what are you doing?"

"She said, 'Brother Schambach told me if I would praise the Lord until my head hit the pillow, I would wake up seeing. And I've got perfect sight for the first time in 24 years.'

"We didn't eat breakfast. We had church in the kitchen. We stood there and I looked up to God and said, 'Lord, if You can heal Mama's eyes, You can pay the rent. Take Your time, You've got two hours yet.'"

Isn't that beautiful? Last night she was bawling and squalling. Now it's down to two hours and she's saying, "Take Your time, Lord." When God does something for you personally, you trust Him to do something greater all the time.

At 8:30 a.m. the mailman came, and she said, "Oh, this must be it!" When you're trusting God for money, you try to think it through logically. So she ran down and got six envelopes out of the mailbox. But when you're expecting money, nothing seems to come but bills! That's just what happened. No money, just four bills. Now isn't that just like the devil. You're believing God to meet the need and here comes four more bills. But when God opens your blind mama's eyes, you'll believe Him for anything.

She said, "Those bills didn't bother me. I just laid them on the table and said, 'Lord, while You're paying the rent, catch these four while You're at it, too.'" This is the way out.

About 9 o'clock she got a phone call, and there was a woman on the other end of the line. "Hello. Are you Miss So-and-So?"

"Sure am."

My name is Such-and-Such. Do you remember me?"

"Sure don't."

"Well, 16 years ago I borrowed some money from you."

"Oh, now I remember! I know who you are."

The woman said, "Can you come over and get the money? I've got it for you."

"I never thought I would get it back."

"I never thought I would give it back," she said, "but last night something got ahold of me."

Then this woman told how she was window-shopping Sunday night in the loop in Chicago, when an overwhelming power dragged her down State Street to the Pacific Garden Mission. She'd never been in a mission in her life. She sat in the back, and when the man finished preaching, she got up to leave. But the same power that dragged her in, dragged her to the altar, and God saved that woman...just to get her to pay a bill she owed to one of His saints!

As she knelt at that altar, she heard the voice of God say, "Do you remember the money you borrowed from a little woman 16 years ago? I want you to pay it back with six percent interest for all those years."

She said, "Lord, I don't know where to get ahold of her. But I'll find her and send her a check."

God said, "No check — she needs the cash by 10 o'clock in the morning."

God knows your deadline. He knows all about your need and when it's due.

Now look at this! The woman said, "Lord, I don't know where that lady lives." So God gave her a phone number!

The little woman went to pick up the money and got back to her house around 9:45 a.m. The sheriff was waiting to put her out. Imagine what his face looked like when she handed him four months' back rent and four months' rent in advance. And the next night she handed me an envelope with a hundred dollar bill in it!

God will allow you to get into a situation where you have to depend on Him...follow His leading...do what He tells you to do. He is going to make a way where there is no way. The discipline of the winding path.

God is concerned about every one of us. He knows you by name. He knows where you live. He knows your telephone number. He knows your deadline. He knows what you need. And He will not fail you. All He's looking for is a people that will be obedient to Him.

Chapter 2

The Discipline of the Impossible Place

And Moses stretched out his hand over the sea; and the Lord caused the sea to go back by a strong east wind all that night, and made the sea dry land, and the waters were divided.   And the children of Israel went into the midst of the sea upon the dry ground: and the waters were a wall unto them on their right hand, and on their left (Exodus 14:21,22).

The children of Israel were facing an impossible situation. Here they were at the Red Sea, the impossible place — and Pharaoh was running after them. But God was at work in their behalf, preparing to reverse the thing — turn it around for their good.

When you are in an impossible situation, don't back up. Don't turn and detour to the side. Make sure you always go forward and God will provide a miracle for you. What you can't do, God will do for you. He'll make a way where there is no way.

You may be in an impossible situation now. But I want you to know, God is going to reverse it and turn the thing around. Your way out is already assured. God leads and guides His people into impossible situations for one reason — so He can get them to trust Him.

God Has a Plan

Several years ago, I held a tent meeting in Pharr, Texas, right on the Mexican border. The opening night we didn't even have the center section filled. And I thought to myself, *Oh, Lord, did I miss Your voice? What in the world am I doing here?*

Then I got word that the mayor was there. I thought maybe he was going to give me the key to the city. Instead he had bad news for me.

He said, "I've come to tell you, you're taking this tent down."

"I just put it up," I said.

The mayor told me he didn't believe in what I was doing.

I told him that's why we came. That's why we put this thing up. We're staying three weeks.

He said, "If you stay, I'll have to arrest you. This is my city."

"Oh," I said, "I've got news for you. This city belongs to my Father. The earth is the Lord's and the fullness thereof. He's called me to preach this Gospel to all the world. And I'm going to preach."

"If you preach," he threatened, "I'll arrest you."

I told him to do what he had to do. I'd do what I had to do.

Well, you can imagine what happened next. Two gentlemen met me at the close of that service with a warrant for my arrest. They said the charge was preaching the Gospel with a loudspeaker. Sure enough, I was guilty.

They took me down before the judge — a woman. She asked, "How do you plead?"

I answered, "Guilty, your honor. I'm guilty of preaching the Gospel with a loudspeaker."

"Then," she said, "the fine is $52.50."

"Oh," I said, "that's cheap enough." I paid her off in nickels. That's about all the Mexican people in that area had been able to put in the offering — nickels!

The next day I found myself wondering why. *Why did I have to suffer the indignity of being arrested? Why did I have to stand before a judge?* Then I remembered that Jesus stood before a judge, and I'm certainly no better than He is. Even Paul found himself in jail more than he did in the pulpit! When he went to town, he didn't look for the local Holiday Inn, he wanted to find out where the jail was. He knew he was going to end up there sooner or later. Still I wondered why. But I didn't have to wonder for very long.

Guess what? The very next day they had my picture on the front page of the newspaper along with the story of my arrest. Free advertising! I couldn't afford any ads so God allowed me to get arrested so they would give me $150,000 worth of advertising. Eyewitness News came on at 6:00 p.m. and they put me on there for eight minutes. There was another half million dollars worth!

I got to the tent that night and you couldn't get near the thing. It was filled to capacity. And God told me, "You couldn't draw the crowd, but I'll draw the crowd for you. If you'll lift Me up, I'll draw all men unto Me."

God had a plan all the time. I gave an altar call that second night and 1,000 people came to get saved.

"Oh," I said, "devil, you ain't got no sense! Go ahead, let them arrest me again."

So they arrested me the second night. I'm on the front page of the paper again the next day. I'm dominating Eyewitness News. The tent is running over, people standing outside. I didn't wonder why anymore!

Revival broke out. They arrested me four nights in a row. The judge took $10,000 of God's money.

We went on to Phoenix, Arizona, to preach and when we came back, we ended up in the courtroom again. It took another judge two days to hear the case. Then he called the mayor up before his bench and said, "Mr. Mayor, you arrested this preacher falsely for four straight nights. If you have a law that says he can't preach the Gospel with a loudspeaker, I order you to take that law off your books. He can preach the Gospel anywhere he wants to. You've taken $10,000 of this man's money and I order you to pay it back, every dime."

I didn't feel right about keeping that money when I got it back. So you know what I did with it? I bought some property in Texas, opened a Bible College, and started training students how to preach the Gospel with a loudspeaker! The devil's got no sense. Instead of just one Schambach, now there are hundreds like me running around the country telling about the Good News.

Stop wondering why. God's not done with you yet. He's going to turn things around and get you out of that impossible situation.

Jesus is With You in the Impossible Place

All through the history of the Church you will find God leading His people into seemingly impossible situations.

Look at Shadrach, Meshach, and Abednego in Daniel 3. A decree came forth from King Nebuchadnezzar that at the sound of music, every knee had to bow and pay homage to the god he had created with his own hands. Everybody was bowing down — even all of God's people, except three. Thank God for three.

They said, "We're not going to bow down to

any false god. There's only one God. And He is the only One that we're going to serve."

These three men were mayors of certain provinces in Babylon. But they were taken captive when the king got word they were not bowing down to his god. He ordered them to be brought before him.

He said, "I've heard some bad news about you. I hear that you're not bowing down when you hear the music."

"That's right, king," they said. "There's only one God, and He's the only One we're going to worship."

The king commanded them again to bow down and worship. "I'm the king," he said, "and if you don't bow down like I've ordered, you'll burn."

The three men laughed, "You've got it backwards, king. If we bow down, we will burn — not in your furnace but another one. And if we've got to choose furnaces, we'll choose yours. We're going to serve God."

This made the king angry. He commanded his servants to heat the furnace seven times hotter. He didn't know it but he was playing right into the hands of God. Nebuchadnezzar was putting the Hebrew children into an impossible place.

"I'll give you one more chance," said the king. "Bow down!"

"Nothing doing, king. God is able to deliver us out of your furnace. He's going to deliver us out of your hands."

When God heard them say that, He said to Jesus, "Get on down there and get in that fire!"

The guards who picked the three men up bodily and tossed them into the furnace could not stand the intensity of the heat — they died on the spot.

The king came over, looked in, and saw the Hebrew children shouting and dancing in the flames with their clothes unburnt. He said, "I see four of them. And the fourth One is like unto the Son of God."

I tell you, it *was* the Son of God. He was in that furnace with them. He made a way where there was no way! Jesus came right into that impossible situation, knocked the "i-m" off of it, and made all things possible to them that believed.

It's Time to Trust God

Look at 1 Samuel 11. This chapter is a message in itself.

Nahash is the enemy, the Ammonite. I don't even like the sound of his name — Nahash.

Nahash the Ammonite came up, and encamped against Jabesh-gilead: and all the men of Jabesh said unto Nahash, Make a covenant with us, and we will serve thee (vs. 1). They got into an impossible situation.

Nahash told them he would help them on one condition. He said, "I'll thrust out all your right eyes and lay it for a reproach upon all Israel."

How do you like that? "I'll help you but I want your right eye." Hear me, beloved. You go to the devil for help and he won't be satisfied with an

eye. He'll want an eye, an ear, an arm, and a leg.
Before long he'll want your life — he'll kill you before
it's over.

The elders said, "Give us seven days to think
about this thing." And they sent to Saul for help.

Saul rallied all the Church around them. He
said to the men who came from Jabesh-gilead, "Go
back and tell those people that on the seventh day, by
the time the sun is hot, they'll have help."

Now it's time to trust God. God is going to
perform a miracle...by the time the sun is hot. God
knows how much you can stand. God knows how
much you can bear. He knows how much pressure
you can take. And with that temptation, with that test,
with that trial, He will make a way of escape. Mark
it down in your Bible that there is a way out of your
dilemma!

Once when I went into a hospital to pray for a
lady, doctors told me that any other woman would
have been dead two weeks ago. I said, "You hit it on
the head, Doc. She's not some other woman. She is
a child of God. A child of God can stand a little more
pain. A child of God can stand a little more pressure.
Why? Because she's got Somebody on the inside of
her. Jesus is here in this hospital room."

He's there with you in the midst of trouble. He
said, "When you go through the water, the water will
not overflow you. When you go through the fire, you
shall not be burned" (see Isaiah 43:2). Why?
"Because I am there with you in the fire and I will
lead you out of this impossible situation. You're
coming out victoriously." That's the Good News!

The pressure may be getting to you. The heat is getting insufferable. You're looking for a way out. I have the secret to your way out. The way out is Jesus Christ!

If you're in an impossible place, God will bring you out of it. At one time or another, we all find ourselves in an impossible place. You may be there financially. You may be there domestically. The devil might have succeeded in breaking up your home. You may even have the divorce papers in your hand. But I want you to know there is a way out. God's never too late.

Jesus is Your Way Out

Look at King Hezekiah. I love this old boy. Here comes the Prophet Isaiah marching right into the bed chamber of the king, unannounced. He doesn't come in saying, "God save the king."

He comes into the king's chambers and there announces, "Thus saith the Lord, 'set your house in order. You're going to die and not live'" (see 2 Kings 20). Didn't even say good-bye, just turned around and walked out.

That's an impossible place.

Hezekiah turns his face to the wall and begins to pray. He begins to cry out to God. He said, "Lord, You know I've been serving You all the days of my life." (He had to be lying in his teeth. If he was serving God, how come God sent a prophet to tell him to set his house in order? It must have been out of order.)

All he could see when he turned his face to the wall was his own reflection. You want to see how good you are? Look in the mirror. If you want to see how bad you look, get a glimpse of Jesus. Then you'll see nothing good in yourself.

Finally Hezekiah rolled over and looked up. When he did, he saw Jesus. He started to repent before God and said, "Lord, the dead can't praise you, only the living can. So I'm going to praise You, Lord. Hallelujah. Glory to God. My iniquity is gone. You have forgiven me."

Praise will move God to action. You want to get an answer from Him? Praise Him.

Isaiah was going out that second gate. God nudged him on the shoulder and said, "Stop. Turn around, go back in there, and tell that king I saw his tears and I've heard his prayer. Tell him he isn't going to die. I'm going to give him 15 more years."

No matter how impossible your situation may seem to be, God is going to bring you out of it. It may look like there's no hope, no way out. But I want you to know Jesus is the way out.

When I get to Heaven, I sure want to talk to Lazarus and ask him some questions. The first million years I'm going to sit down with Jesus, then I want to go talk with Lazarus and find out what it was like to be dead, wrapped up in that tomb. You talk about an impossible situation!

Jesus got a letter from Mary and Martha that read, "He whom thou lovest is sick. Come and heal him."

Jesus said, "I'm not going anywhere." And He waited until Lazarus died and was in the grave four days.

Now, he had raised a young girl from the dead and the unbelievers just scoffed and said she must have just been in a coma. He raised the widow of Nain's son up from the funeral procession and people said he was in a prolonged coma. *Jesus thought, Wait until next time, I'll fix them.*

He waited until Lazarus died, until they had put him in the grave for four days — decomposition had set in, the flesh was going back to dust.

Then Jesus said to His disciples, "Let's go, boys. Lazarus is asleep and I'm going to wake him up."

The disciples weren't too thrilled with the idea. "Lord, let the man sleep. We're tired, too — the way You hold these meetings, You keep us until after midnight. Let the man rest."

But Jesus kept on. "Lazarus is dead, let's go raise him from the dead."

He was talking to men who were healing the sick and casting out devils, but they couldn't believe that Jesus had power to raise the dead. This is an impossible place.

Jesus comes on the scene. Martha was the first one to see Him. She fell at His feet and said, "Lord, if You'd been here four days ago, my brother wouldn't have died."

Isn't that just like some folks? She had faith for four days ago, but not for today. In other words, she was saying, "You're too late." But God is never too late!

Jesus said, "Martha, your brother's going to rise again." She didn't catch on because she replied, "I know he will at the Resurrection in the last day."

See how her faith jumped from four days ago to the last day? But she still didn't have any faith for today! She was just like some church folks are today. You ask them, "Do you believe in Jesus?"

"Yes, He died on the cross."

"Do you really believe in Jesus?"

"Yes, He's coming again. He died 2,000 years ago, but He's coming again."

"What's He doing now?"

"Oh, He's sitting on a cloud, playing a harp." Do you see why we have trouble getting God to answer us?

Jesus said to Lazarus' family and friends, "Show Me where you've laid him."

He stood in front of that grave site. It looked impossible. And then He commanded, "Roll the stone away."

That got to me. If He could get Lazarus out of the grave, don't you think He could have rolled that stone away? Then how come He's asking them to roll the stone away? Because God won't do anything for you that you can do for yourself. You do what you can do, and then He'll do what you can't do.

Martha came and said, "Lord, he's been in there four days. He stinks by now!"

Have you ever had people tell you, "It's alright to get religious, but you don't have to get fanatical about it"?

Jesus said, "Didn't I tell you that if you would believe you'd see the glory of God? Now roll that thing away."

He stands in front of that tomb and yells, "LAZARUS!"

And I can picture the Jews standing there, saying, "Oh, Lord, Jesus is trying to call him out."

And they murmur among themselves, "Do you think he's coming out?"

"No, sir. I put him in there. He's dead."

"But He's the blind man Healer."

"I know it. But them blind folks had breath in their lungs. That man ain't got no breath. He ain't coming out of there."

"What's that noise?"

Jesus yells, "LAZARUS, COME OUT!" And here comes Lazarus bouncing out of there. Hallelujah!

I tell you there's a way out of your trouble. There's a way out of your dilemma. There's a way out of your sickness. There's a way out of your disease. Jesus is the way out of every impossible situation and today is your day for a miracle! Hallelujah!

I'm reminded of the testimony of a beautiful, 17-year-old girl with tuberculosis. One lung had collapsed, the other one was half gone. She was a Nazarene, beautifully saved. She loved Jesus with all her heart.

But her pastor didn't believe in divine healing. I'm not putting him down — I don't put people down because they don't believe in healing. Healing doesn't unite us and make us one — the blood makes us one.

And if you're washed in the blood, you're my brother whether you like it or not. We are kinfolk. But if your church doesn't believe in divine healing, you're getting shorted.

That young girl's doctor was a Christian man, but he couldn't do a thing for her. She wasted away from 120 pounds to about 60 pounds. Medically, there was no hope.

Her doctor said, "I'm sending you home to die. I don't tell everybody this, but you're a Christian and there is no death to the child of God. You'll just go on home to be with Jesus." And that's true.

That girl went home and spent her time in an oxygen tent, breathing pure oxygen 24 hours a day. They had her propped up inside so she could read her Bible.

One day she was reading in the first of Peter's epistles: *Who his own self bare our sins in his own body on the tree, that we, being dead to sins, should live unto righteousness...* (vs. 24). She stopped and laid the Bible down, put her hands up, with tears falling from her eyes, and said, "Oh, Jesus, I'm so glad I'm saved. I'm not afraid of death because there is no death. There is a transition — to be absent from the body — but I'll be present with You. Oh," she said, "I'll be so glad to see You."

Seventeen years of age. She's never been taught the truth of healing. So she praised God for salvation for 20 minutes and finally got back into her Bible and started where she left off. *Who his own self bare our sins in his own body on the tree, that we, being dead to sins, should live unto* *righteousness...*this time she didn't stop. It's the same verse...*by whose stripes ye were healed.*

She said right out loud, "Oh, my God, look what I found!"

There was no preacher around...no mother around. She was alone with her Bible and she got a revelation on healing.

She put her hands up again, "Lord, I just praised You for the first part of that verse. Now I'm going to praise You for the last part of it. It's like a neon sign has flashed on for me — by whose stripes you were healed. Hallelujah, I thank You that You said I'm healed! It's already accomplished! Devil, you're a liar, I'm well. I'm healed by His stripes."

She unzipped that oxygen tent, mustered all the lung power she could and hollered, "Mama, come quick!"

Mama came stumbling up the stairs. She ran in and saw her daughter sitting with her scrawny legs out over the side of that bed. Mama needed a doctor now! She gasped, "What is it, child?"

"Oh, Mama, read what I found. Look! Read what I found!"

Mama said, "Lay down, girl."

"I will after you read what I've found. Don't you see what it says? It says I was healed by His stripes. Mama, I'm not going to die!"

Mama started crying now —WAAAAAAAAA!

"What are you crying for?" the girl asked.

"Because the doctor said the day you died you'd probably lose your mind."

Now, isn't that strange? If you're willing to

keep the sickness, you're in your normal mind. But when you're believing God for healing, you've lost your mind. That's the way the world looks at it.

She said, "Mama, I'm not losing my mind. I'm in my right mind for the first time. God says I'm healed. I'll have two eggs over medium, hash brown potatoes, a glass of orange juice, and coffee."

"WAAAAAAAAAAAAAA," Mama's still crying. "You haven't eaten anything in 12 months. Now I know you've lost your mind."

Mama tucked her back in and zipped up the oxygen tent. But that precious girl sneaked out of the room!

When her mother went out and closed the door, she unzipped the tent, pulled her legs out over the side of the bed, got up and went to her closet. She put on one of the dresses she used to wear when she weighed 120 pounds, put her slippers on her feet, and went downstairs.

She opened the kitchen door, and when Mama saw her, she almost fainted.

"Is my breakfast ready?" the girl asked.

Her mother made her breakfast, all the time staring at her daughter. She took the plate of food to her, and the daughter bowed her head and said, "Lord, I thank You for this food for my brand-new body. Bless it in the name of Jesus."

Oh, one more thing. Do you know what this girl said to the Lord when she found the scripture that taught her about healing? She said, "Oh, Jesus, I'm sorry to tell You this, but I won't be coming home right away. I'm going to be staying around here a while longer since I found out Your Word says that You carried my sickness for me!"

She went to the doctor the next day and they found two brand-new lungs in her body. Hallelujah! That girl is still alive today. She lives in New York City — has given birth to four children.

Remember, this girl was in an impossible place. She didn't have a pastor, she didn't have an evangelist, she didn't even have a mother to stand with her in prayer. You don't need anybody else. All you need is the Word of God. You can stand on that Word. Let every man and every devil be a liar, but let God be true!

I want to stress to you that if you're sick or diseased or afflicted, God had nothing to do with that sickness. God had nothing to do with that disease. The devil put it on you. But I want to preach some Good News to you. Jesus is going to take it off of you. You don't have to stay in that condition. You don't have to stay sick or diseased or afflicted because He said, *I am the Lord that healeth thee* (Exodus 15:26). Hallelujah!

Chapter 3

The Discipline of the Bitter Place

So Moses brought Israel from the Red sea, and they went out into the wilderness of Shur; and they went three days in the wilderness, and found no water. And when they came to Marah, they could not drink of the waters of Marah, for they were bitter: therefore the name of it was called Marah. And the people murmured against Moses, saying, What shall we drink?...and the Lord shewed him a tree, which when he had cast into the waters, the waters were made sweet... (Exodus 15:22-25).

Nobody likes to be disciplined. It is against our nature...it goes against the flesh...we don't like to be told what to do. Someone says, "Hey, man, I'm free."

That's what you think. God said, "You have not chosen Me, but I have chosen you. I have called you, and I have ordained you." The bottom line of this whole Christian life is for you and me as children of God to be led by the Holy Spirit.

This is where discipline comes in. If you won't submit to the discipline of God, then you'll end up being led by a human being. And if you follow some men's advice, you could end up like the thousand folks who followed the Jim Jones cult and died in Guyana. Do you see what I'm getting at? If you're going to follow somebody, then look unto Jesus who is the Author and Finisher of your faith. You need to be led by His Spirit.

God's trying to get us to the place where we can learn how to trust Him. That's what faith means. Faith is believing God. Faith is trusting God. Real faith is following Jesus and doing what He tells you to do.

Now here's a simple definition of faith. I call it, "the ABCs of faith." Faith is an *Action*, based upon a *Belief* that is supported by *Confidence*.

You and I provide the action. First, read the Word. Find a promise in the Bible and then put your faith to work by saying, "If God said it, He'll do it. And if He spoke it, He will bring it to pass. I believe God. I believe He will do what He said."

A Special Kind of Discipline

Do you ever wonder why you pray for an

answer and things sometimes get worse?

Now I want to tell you about a special kind of discipline — the discipline of the bitter place.

Not everything in life is sweet. Oh, we thought it would be. We thought after we got saved that everything would be sweet, but we soon run into a lot of bitter things. But you don't have to stay in that bitterness. God has a way out. And He has a formula to turn bitter waters into sweet waters.

God led His people out of Egypt's bondage — out onto the winding path of the wilderness, out from underneath the whiplash of Pharaoh.

Then He led them through the impossible place. We saw how they were boxed in by the Red Sea, and God performed a miracle so they crossed over on dry ground. Pharaoh and his army with its horses and chariots followed after them. But the waters came back together and all the soldiers and horses were drowned in the sea.

God may allow you to get into an impossible place. But He has a way of turning the thing around and working it out for your good.

After being delivered from their impossible place, the children of Israel went on their journey to the Promised Land. Oh, they were expecting paradise, a land flowing with milk and honey. But they soon discovered that Canaan is not Heaven. It's a place of victory where you put the devil under your feet, where you can move in and lay claim to the promises of God while you are living right here on planet Earth.

So now the Israelites are on the journey to their place of victory and inheritance. They go three days and there is no water. On the third day they found water, but it was bitter and they couldn't drink it.

Now, they were made out of the same stuff you and I are made out of, so they started to complain and to murmur — not only against Moses, but against God. "What are we going to drink? Why did you bring us out here in the desert to die of thirst?"

This was their first test after the victory at the Red sea. It was a new trial of faith. What a shock to find that the Promised Land was not a smiling paradise, but a dreary wilderness.

You may have thought when you got saved that everything was going to be peaches and cream. But now you've found out all Hell has broken loose against you, and there are some bitter things following you around. And now you may be asking, "What am I going to do?"

I promise you — God will come into that situation, sweeten the trial, and bring victory to you.

You're a child of God, and your only Source of comfort and advice is Jesus.

When trials come into your life, do not seek the advice that you used to seek before. Don't rely on magazines, advice columns, or horoscopes. I hear a lot of Christian people talking about astrology, going back to the stars. You're not of those people that study stars. You're a child of God — the One who put the stars in place.

Learn to Depend on God

God doesn't want you to use the implements of the devil as your guide for living. He has a better plan and a better purpose for you because you are His child. God doesn't want us to put our trust in men or human organizations. He wants us to follow Him. He is the only One Who can satisfy the longing desire of your soul.

Many times God allows us to get into difficult situations just to show us our utter dependence on Him. You cannot be satisfied with the things that come out of the earth.

The children of Israel wanted water. Water is a natural thing. Everybody needs it to live. If you don't put water in your body, eventually it will die.

So Moses ... *cried unto the Lord; and the Lord shewed him a tree, which when he had cast into the waters, the waters were made sweet: there he made for them a statute and an ordinance, and there he proved them* (Exodus 15:25).

The word *proved* means "testing" their commitment. Are you committed to God? People today — especially the youth — are looking for something to be committed to. But too many in the church are not committed to Christ. Are you listening to me? Children see that their parents — their own father and mother — aren't even committed to each other. So why should they be committed to Christ?

God is looking for men and women who will be committed to Him no matter what kind of trial or test comes. Make a commitment that doesn't look to your own natural resources, but unto God! He's the One Who led you out of bondage and He's the One Who will lead you to your full inheritance in Christ Jesus. Hallelujah!

You've got to realize that God doesn't always remove the bitter place. When trouble comes, the first thing we want to do is have surgery — get rid of it. But surgery isn't the answer all the time.

God provided for the Israelites. They found water. But it was bitter. He was testing their faith. Then He sweetened the trial and made the bitter waters sweet. He didn't give them another body of water. He told them, "There's a tree standing there. Throw it in the waters and it will sweeten them."

God has a way even though you're in a mess. He's got a way of coming into that mess and causing the mess to get sweet. Isn't that beautiful?

We're always looking for a way out. "How can I get out of this mess?" Stay in it and dangle a while. God is a specialist in making the bitter waters sweet.

I think you know what I'm talking about. There are situations in your life that seem like a bitter pill to swallow. Well, wrap Jesus around the pill and you'll be able to swallow the thing because He knows how to make those bitter things sweet.

Swallow the Pill of Forgiveness

Have you ever wondered why some people aren't healed?

I had some ladies in my church once who came wanting prayer for a miracle but they never did get healed. Finally I found out why.

I'd notice how they wouldn't talk to one another. One woman came in and looked over the congregation. When she saw a particular woman sitting on one side, she'd sit on the other side. These two "saints" wouldn't talk to each other but they sure made a lot of noise. They shouted and danced and whooped but they wouldn't talk to one another. Then they'd come through the prayer line and expect to get healed. But they never did get anything.

One day I had a bread-breaking service and I went down and got one of those women by the hand.

She said, "Praise the Lord, Brother Schambach."

I grabbed her by the hand and started off. "Come with me, girl." And I went to the other side. When the other lady saw me coming, she started to leave.

I said, "Hold it. I'm getting you two together. I'm tired of this feuding right in church. How in the world can you say you love God when you can't love somebody you see right in the flesh? You have got to make this thing right or you'll never go to Heaven. You'll die and go to Hell!"

I had the women embrace, and I saw boo-hooing and crying. One said, "Forgive me, it's my fault," and the other one said, "No, it ain't your fault, it's my fault."

I said, "Don't fight again. My God, just kiss and make up!"

When they embraced each other, one of them lost a tumor — a 15-pound growth just disintegrated. The other lady was healed of heart disease. Why? Because they got together. They made a bitter situation sweet. I promise that when you get Jesus in that bitter situation, He'll turn it around and make the bitter waters sweet.

No Color to God

How in the world can we say we love God and not love one another?

Some white folks can't even love black folks. And that goes the other way, too. Some black folks don't love white folks either. But when you get saved, you find out there's no color to God. There's no male or female to God. There's no bond or free to God.

I remember holding a meeting in Atlanta, Georgia in 1960. Some people came to the meeting and wanted me to put a line down the center to separate the races. I said, "No way. We're not going to do that!" We just let everybody sit and worship God together. And revival broke out. White folks started hugging black folks. Black folks started hugging white folks.

Then the Ku Klux Klan came out. They called me at my motel and said, "You're a dead man if you hold meetings out there tonight." I told the caller that I was already dead.

"Who are you?" I asked.

"I'm the head of the Ku Klux Klan," he said.

"Well, I don't know who you are," I said, "but my Head's in Heaven. His name is Jesus."

He didn't let up so easily. "If you go out there tonight, we'll carry you out of this city in a casket."

So I got tough. "I said I'm already dead. And before you can get to me, you've got to walk all over the Father's hand. You've got to break the seal of the Holy Ghost, and you've got to come through Jesus. I'm crucified with Christ." I hung up the phone and went to the service.

A hundred of the Ku Klux Klan were sitting in the back of the tent that night. They had bicycle chains, knives, and guns. The Holy Ghost came on me and I went back there and preached to them. I looked them eyeball to eyeball, and I preached from the Book of Jude. When I gave an altar call, 75 of those 100 dropped their guns and other weapons and ran to the altar to get saved! Hallelujah!

Jesus Went Through Your Experience

After one of Jesus' greatest experiences, being baptized in water, the Holy Ghost came on Him in the form of a dove. The Father's voice said, "This is my beloved Son, in whom I am well pleased."

Jesus fasted for 40 days and 40 nights, and THEN the Bible says, He was led of the Spirit. Where? Into the wilderness to be tempted of the devil.

So when you end up in the bitter place, remember that Jesus isn't asking you to do something He didn't do. He went through it. He was tested and yet overcame the devil. You and I have the same weapon that Jesus had at His disposal — the Word of God. You can confront the devil on the same grounds.

The devil hates you. The Bible says that the thief comes to kill, to steal, and to destroy. You may find yourself looking at him eyeball to eyeball. But the devil cannot kill you because your life is hid with Christ in God.

I don't care what you're called to go through. Don't ask God to take you out of it. He will come right into that situation, sweeten it, and make a way where there is no way.

Stay where you are. It may be bitter right now, but when you invite God to come into that place, He will make it a place of sweetness.

Saul of Tarsus became the Apostle Paul, one of the greatest apostles who ever lived. Because he was preaching the Gospel, he and Silas were thrown into jail. But that dungeon became a sanctuary of holy song and praises to God.

At midnight, they were inside that jail, bound hand and foot. They weren't exactly weeping tears of joy. Then Silas asked Paul, "What do we do now?"

He said, "It's time to sing songs of victory."

Some people can't even sing in church, let alone sing in the midst of a trial. But if you'll ask, Jesus Christ will make an entrance into that situation and turn it around 180 degrees. You'll be on the top instead of being on the bottom.

God is concerned about you and everything you're going through. He cares about the tests you're going through in your family relationships, in your home, with your son or daughter. You may think you're being ill-treated at home, but don't run. Stay there.

Young people tell me, "I'm the only one saved in the house. What am I going to do?"

And I ask them, "What do you think He saved you first for? You're the worst one of the bunch. And if God can save the worst, He's going to save the rest of them!"

Hang in there, husband. Hang in there, wife. Hang in their, brother. Hang in there, sister. If God can save you, He can save anybody. Stay in that situation. God will turn it around. He'll take the bitterness out of it and make it sweet.

There was a tree growing by the bitter waters of Marah long before Moses and the Israelites got there. But when God used that tree, something happened. The bitter waters became sweet. That tree is a type of Calvary. The cross of Calvary covers it all. If you bring the cross into every situation, God will take the most hardened sinner and make a saint out of him. He will take a harlot off the street and make a lovely woman out of her; as pure as if she'd never sinned before. He'll take drug addicts and alcoholics, save them and send them out as His ministers to this generation.

The Branch of Healing

God always puts the branch of healing beside every spring of sorrow. Perhaps you are going through sorrow right now. Let me tell you — there already stands the branch of healing — the Tree of Promise, the Word of Life. It will open up fountains in the desert. Songs will break forth in the night.

Many times we are in darkness. We can't see the way out. But God turns on the light and shows us the way out of that situation. He'll always use something that's in the same situation you are. Right there within reach, you'll find your miracle. Hallelujah!

The Lord showed Moses the tree. So Moses decided to make a covenant with God's people and said, *If thou wilt diligently hearken to the voice of the Lord thy God, and wilt do that which is right in his sight, and wilt give ear to his commandments, and keep all his statutes, I will put none of these diseases upon thee, which I have brought upon the Egyptians: for I am the Lord that healeth thee* (Exodus 15:26, emphasis mine).

God made a covenant with His people. He brought them out of bondage, out of captivity. In the Psalms it says that out of three and a half million people, not one of them came out with sickness! There wasn't one feeble person among them. When God brought them out of bondage and out of captivity, He brought them out healed.

No sooner were they out on the other side of the Red sea and on their journey, when God meets with them and establishes the covenant of healing.

If your church doesn't believe in healing, get out of it. You are missing one of the greatest blessings God ever gave to the Church. God made a covenant with His people and established a statute of healing. It's right there in the Word! Then why don't we accept divine healing?

Every promise you find in the Bible has a hinge on it — a hinge of condition — something you've got to do. How in the world can you believe that God is your Healer if you're not obeying Him? He said, "You walk in My ways, you keep My statutes, and all My commandments." When we do what He says we're supposed to do, we have the promise. This is the condition.

If you're a child of God, walking in His way, He'll hear you when you pray. When you ask God for something, you can be confident He'll give it to you. With that kind of confidence you can come to God and ask Him what you want, and you'll walk out with your miracle.

The ordinance of divine healing that God placed in the Church has never been revoked. I'm not the healer, Jesus is the Healer. Schambach couldn't heal a flea if it had a headache.

If you are sick or diseased and afflicted, I have good news for you. Your elder Brother carried that sickness in His own body 2,000 years ago and He wants you well. This is your day for a miracle. Allow God to turn the bitterness of sickness into the sweetness of health for you today!

Chapter 4

The Discipline of the Hungry Place

And they took their journey from Elim, and all the congregation of the children of Israel came unto the wilderness of Sin, which is between Elim and Sinai, on the fifteenth day of the second month after their departing out of the land of Egypt. And the whole congregation of the children of Israel murmured against Moses and Aaron in the wilderness: And the children of Israel said unto them, Would to God we had died by the hand of the Lord in the land of Egypt, when we sat by the flesh pots, and when we did eat bread to the full; for ye have brought us forth into this wilderness, to kill this whole assembly with hunger (Exodus 16:1-3).

When God brings you out of sin — out from under the whiplash of Pharaoh, out of trouble — He brings you out for one purpose. He wants to move you into the place that He has already provided for you, a place of completeness. God wants you well. He wants you blessed. He wants your needs met.

He said, "All of these blessings shall come upon you, and they shall overtake you. I will bless you in the city, and I will bless you in the country. I'll bless your basket. I'll bless your store. I'll bless the fruit of your womb. I'll bless your seed. Everything you set your hands to, I will bless it. I will make you the head and not the tail. You shall lend and not borrow" (see Deuteronomy 28). This is what God intends for every one of us.

Now there are times we get involved in situations we don't have any business being in. Sometimes we get in a mess because of our own ingenuity. We made a wrong move or a wrong decision. And as a result, things get tight. We exhaust our supplies. We have to tighten our belt to the last notch — and then some. But even then God's not going to leave you. He's going to come into that situation and turn it around and work it for your good.

"What Is It?"

Let's rejoin the children of Israel as they're wandering in the wilderness. By now the people are murmuring and complaining because they're hungry.

They're crying for some bread. "If you don't feed me, I'm going to start growling — and not just my stomach!"

They said, "Would to God He would have killed us back there in Egypt when we were by the flesh pots. At least we had something to eat back there."

Now remember, these are God's people complaining. God delivered them from Pharaoh's hand, performed the miracle at the Red Sea...and they're worried about whether they'll eat or not!

So Moses gets on his face before God and says, "Lord, do You hear that?"

God says, "What do you think? They're not complaining against you. They're complaining against me. You tell them that I will miraculously provide for them."

You see, God drove them into the wilderness to test them, to prove them. The word *prove* in our King James Version means "to test." This is the discipline of the hungry place.

The Lord told Moses, "You tell them I'm going to pour out manna on them in the morning. I will supply their needs."

Do you know what *manna* means in the Hebrew? It means, "What is it?" That's literally what it means. When the Israelites got up the next morning, they cried out, "What is it?" And Moses said, "That's it!" They couldn't even name the thing!

They didn't have to work for it. God provided it for them fresh every morning in the exact amount needed for each day. He gave it to them six days a week and on the sixth day, He provided a double portion so they wouldn't have to work on the seventh day. It was the Sabbath — the Lord's day.

God allowed them to get into a situation where they had to trust Him. They were being conditioned for the miraculous. This didn't go on just for a week or a month, but for 40 years. Forty years!

"Give Us More!"

Then the children complained again and said, "Lord, we're getting tired of this bread. We want some meat."

And God said, "Moses, tell them I'll rain quail on them at night."

Now, isn't that just like God? The first thing He did was give them carbohydrates for the body, then He gave them some protein to go along with it! He wanted them to have a sound body to go with a sound mind.

God was trying to tell the people they couldn't get along with just earthly sustenance. Oh, thank God for the Quarter Pounders, but they are only good for the body. You need something for the soul. And that something can only come from God. You can't get it from your church. You can't get it from a good song. You can't get it from a fried chicken dinner in the church parlor. You can't get it from man-made things. It takes something supernatural to satisfy the longing desire of your spirit.

The world can't satisfy you. You may feel like

an illegitimate child sometimes because you're not accepted by either the world or the church. It will be that way if you've got one foot in the world and one foot in the church. You've got to come out from the world and be separated.

God delivered the children of Israel from Egypt, which is a type of the world. And God brought you out of the world — saved you, cleaned you up. Now the only thing that can satisfy you is the supernatural power of the living God.

The Apostle Paul says in the tenth chapter of 1 Corinthians: *Moreover, brethren, I would not that ye should be ignorant, how that all our fathers were under the cloud, and all passed through the sea; And were all baptized unto Moses in the cloud and in the sea; And did all eat the same spiritual meat* (vss. 1-3)

Three and a half million people all ate the same spiritual meat. What was it? Manna! Isn't it amazing that God would provide something *supernatural* to sustain His people?

Here they are, a short time out of Egypt. Do you remember how they came out? All it took was one miracle.

God said to take a lamb, a lamb for every house. The Israelites were to slit the throat of the lamb and drain the blood into a basin. Then they were to take some hyssop, dip it into the blood, and sprinkle the blood of the lamb on the doorposts and on the lentils of their houses. The death angel was coming through the land to slay the firstborn of every household, human and animal as well.

But God provided protection for His people.

He told them to stay under the protection of the blood, and then take a lamb and roast it. They were to stay inside their houses and eat the roast lamb.

That lamb is typical of the spotless Lamb of God who died on Calvary 2,000 years ago! Do you remember that the Bible says that three and a half million people came out of bondage and captivity, and there wasn't one feeble person among them? No sickness.   No disease!   When God provides deliverance for His people, He provides deliverance for the whole man: body, soul, and spirit.

The reason the children of Israel came out with no sickness and disease is because they ate roast lamb all night long! Now don't go running down to your supermarket to buy a leg of lamb. I'm not talking about that. Jesus is the Lamb of God. He is the only One who can heal your body. He is the only One who can set you free. He is still Jehovah-Jireh, "the Lord will provide."

God is concerned about every one of His people. And there is enough of Jesus to go around for everybody.

Jesus Is the Bread From Heaven

Jesus said He is the Bread from Heaven. "Your fathers ate bread in the wilderness and they are dead," He said, "but if you will eat this Bread you will never die."

Jesus is trying to tell us that He is the "What is it?" — the manna from Heaven! He is the only Source of spiritual strength. Buddha is not the way. Mohammed is not the way. Hare Krishna is not the way. Mr. Moon is not the way. The virgin Mary is not the way. Jesus said, "I am the Way, the Truth, and the Life. And no man comes to the Father but by Me."

Jesus' disciples, when He told them that they had to eat His body at the Last Supper, asked, "How in the world can we eat Him?"

In the beginning was the Word, and the Word was with God, and the Word was God. And the Word was made flesh (John 1:1,14). The Cristos. The Christ. You need to eat the Word. When the doctor says there is no hope, eat the Word. "I am the Lord that healeth thee." The Word became flesh. That is the manna from Heaven. The Lord will sustain you in the hungry place!

Loaves and Fishes

Jesus, during His earthly ministry, was faced with the discipline of the hungry place. He preached to 5,000 men and they were all hungry. And He had preached overtime! He *Himself* knew what He was going to do, but He tried to elicit faith from His disciples. He said, "How much money do we have in the treasury? Not much? Well, we're going to feed the folks." Some of the disciples didn't believe Him.

But here came another disciple, saying, "Lord, here is a lad with five loaves and two fish..." And if he had stopped right there, Jesus would have had a man with some faith. But that man was just like you and me. We don't know when to shut up.

He said, "Here's a boy with five loaves and two fish, BUT..." There we go butting again. We try to be goats instead of sheep. God never intended for us to go around butting. Stop butting the Word of God.

Jesus was not feeding these men just to fill up their bellies. He was using their hunger to demonstrate a truth He wanted to reveal to His disciples, and to us.

Jesus told His disciples to seat the people. Then He took those five loaves and two fish, laid His hands on it, blessed it, and broke it. He gave it to His disciples and told them to serve everybody.

They went through the crowd — those 5,000 men probably had 10,000 women with them and those 10,000 women had 20,000 kids along! But we'll just say 5,000 for the sake of argument.

These adult men, all disciples handpicked by Jesus, served the people. Everybody took a chunk of bread and a chunk of fish. But something unusual was taking place. They couldn't deplete the supply! The more they tore off, the more that came back. Then they started to eat. They couldn't eat it all without more coming back!

The Bible says these men ate until their bellies were full. That's a whole lot of food! When they were through, Jesus told His men to pick up what they didn't eat. They ended up with more than they started with! Well, what was Jesus doing? He was trying to tell them that He was the bread from Heaven! Aren't you glad you are a partaker of that bread from Heaven?

Now look at Exodus 16:12: *I have heard the murmurings of the children of Israel: speak unto them, saying, At even ye shall eat flesh, and in the morning ye shall be filled with bread; and ye shall know that I am the Lord your God.* Verse 35: *And the children of Israel did eat manna forty years, until they came to a land inhabited; they did eat manna, until they came unto the borders of the land of Canaan.*

Jesus Christ, in John 6:26, 27, said, *Verily, verily, I say unto you, Ye seek me, not because ye saw the miracles, but because ye did eat of the loaves, and were filled. Labour not for the meat which perisheth, but for that meat which endureth unto everlasting life, which the Son of man shall give unto you: for him hath God the Father sealed.*

Then said they unto him, What shall we do, that we might work the works of God?

Jesus answered and said unto them, This is the work of God, that ye believe on him whom he hath sent (vss. 28, 29).

There's a great truth! The work of God is to believe on Him whom the Father has sent. That's what Jesus said. That's what the Bible says!

But we can see that the multitudes weren't satisfied with this answer. *They said therefore unto him, What sign shewest thou then, that we may see, and believe thee? what dost thou work? Our fathers did eat manna in the desert; as it is written, He gave them bread from heaven to eat* (vss. 30, 31).

Can you see what they're trying to do? They're saying, "Moses gave our fathers bread to eat all the days of their lives. You give us bread to eat, and then we'll believe You." These people were just like Church people today. They follow Jesus just for the loaves and the fishes. They don't believe Him for the miracles' sake, but because He's feeding their bellies.

Then Jesus said unto them, Verily, verily, I say unto you, Moses gave you not that bread from heaven; but my Father giveth you the true bread from heaven. For the bread of God is he which cometh down from heaven, and giveth life unto the world (vss. 32, 33).

You can be a partaker of that bread from Heaven. God will reach down into the depths of sin, pick you up, wash you in His blood, put a robe of righteousness on you, take out the stony heart, put in a heart of flesh, write your name in the Lamb's Book of Life, and then call you "Son." Oh, hallelujah! I guarantee you He will do it.

You come to Him just like you are, He'll feed you the Bread of Heaven, and you'll never be hungry again!

Chapter 5

The Discipline of the Thirsty Place

And all the congregation of the children of Israel journeyed from the wilderness of Sin, after their journeys, according to the commandment of the Lord, and pitched in Rephidim: and there was no water for the people to drink. Wherefore the people did chide with Moses, and said, Give us water that we may drink. And Moses said unto them, Why chide ye with me? wherefore do ye tempt the Lord? And the people thirsted there for water; and the people murmured against Moses, and said, Wherefore is this that thou hast brought us up out of Egypt, to kill us and our children and our cattle with thirst? And Moses cried unto the Lord, saying, What shall I do unto this people? they be almost ready to stone me.

And the Lord said unto Moses, Go on before the people, and take with thee of the elders of Israel; and thy rod, wherewith thou smotest the river, take in thine hand, and go. Behold, I will stand before thee there upon the rock in Horeb; and thou shalt smite the rock, and there shall come water out of it, that the people may drink. And Moses did so in the sight of the elders of Israel. (Exodus 17:1-6)

There is a discipline of the thirsty place. We're talking about more than just satisfying natural thirst or quenching the thirst of the multitudes. The real issue involves the spiritual thirst of a man's soul.

God demands obedience from every one of us. If necessary, He will allow us to get in situations that force us to obey Him — where if we don't obey Him, then disaster strikes.

God allowed the people of Israel to get into a situation where they had no water. They were out in the middle of the desert, the wilderness. How in the world were they supposed to get water out of sand?

Thank God, He is God! He can do anything! He told Moses to take up his rod — the same rod that got him through the Red sea — and strike a rock. God said, *Behold,* [Moses] *I will stand before thee there upon the rock in Horeb; and thou shalt smite the rock, and there shall come water out of it, that the people may drink. And Moses did so* (vs. 6). This Rock Moses was supposed to go and stand beside is a type of Jesus Christ.

But how was Moses going to get water out of that rock? Here are three and a half million people, crying out for water, ready to stone Moses. He says, "Follow me, we're going to get some spring water."

The people got excited and cried out, "Where?"

"Out of the rock," Moses answered.

"Rock?...Find us some rocks," they screamed. "We'll give you rocks! Stone him!"

But Moses had to obey God. That's why he was the leader. God ordained him to lead the people out of that place.

So Moses, this great man of God, takes the rod, goes to the rock, and strikes it just like God told him to. And all of a sudden that rock starts gushing Perrier! Spring water out of the rock!

Everybody drinks. The cattle drink. They all have a wonderful time of refreshing because Moses did what God told him to do.

I know it sounds crazy. But don't ever try to figure God out. You never will. God takes foolish things to confound the wise.

And often, God will tell you to do things that are contrary to the way you have been educated. It may be against the laws of logic. I don't care whether or not it is logically explainable. Don't try to think it out. If God said do it, then do it.

"Spit in My Eyes!"

One time I was in New York City and a little blind woman came up for prayer. I had about 500 people lined up to pray for but she just came up and stood right in front of me. I put my hands on her and commanded the blind eyes to open. Then I told her to thank God for her sight. I started to lift my hands but she grabbed my arms. She wasn't going to let go!

I said, "Mother, go ahead. Thank God. It's done."

She said, "No, it ain't done."

And I thought, *Oh, no, not one of these.* "Come on, lady, it's done. I prayed for you. God heard us."

But she wasn't letting go! "I'm still blind."

"Mother, will you take it by faith?"

"Brother Schambach, now just be still for a moment. You didn't do what God told me to tell you to do."

"Well, what did God tell you to tell me to do?"

She looked up at me — she couldn't see but she turned those eyes up to where my voice was coming from — and she said, "God told me to tell you to spit in my eyes."

That really got to me. I yelled, "God didn't tell you that, woman. I'm not going to spit in your eyes! It's not sanitary. I won't do it!"

She said, "Oh, yes, you will. 'Cause I ain't moving until you do what God told me to tell you to do."

I tell you, women can be stubborn! So we went back and forth for another minute or so. I kept telling her I was not going to spit in her eyes, and she kept telling me she'd stay there until I did!

I started looking at that long line of people, and I gave in. "All right, I'm going to do it."

I pushed her hair back out of her face and put

both fingers on her eyeballs. Then I pulled the eyelids open. Then...I just couldn't do it.

"I'm not going to do it," I said. "Why don't you just get prayed for like everybody else does?"

"Because God told me to tell you to spit! Are you any better than Jesus?"

I thought, *Oh, Lord, does she know how to hurt a guy! I've read in the Bible where Jesus spit in a man's eyes, and then spat on the ground and made clay and spittle together.* So I said, "All right, I'll do it."

And in front of everybody, I spit in her eyes! When I did, the power of God came on that woman. She had been blind for 28 years, but she ran around that building, completely healed by the power of God. Hallelujah!

Do what He tells you to do! This is what God wants.

He told Moses to strike the rock with the rod. And when he did, water came gushing out...because he obeyed God.

God Will Test Your Obedience

I held a meeting one time and saw a crippled man get up from the invalid section, go over and touch the center pole, and go back to his seat. I thought, *What in the world is he doing?* But when he touched that center pole, he was completely healed by the power of God. God told him to touch the center pole. And he obeyed God. I would have never told him that; God did. God was checking out his obedience.

God will test you in some way. He'll tell you to do something just to see whether or not you'll do it. Before God blesses you with anything else, He may tell you to take $20 down and give it to a poor family. He's preparing a people who will be obedient to His voice. He's looking for people who will obey Him, who will move when He says move, who will do what He says do, and who will stop when He says stop.

Jesus Is the Rock

Look at 1 Corinthians 10:1-4: *Moreover, brethren, I would not that ye should be ignorant, how that all our fathers were under the cloud, and all passed through the sea; And were all baptized unto Moses in the cloud and in the sea; And did all eat the same spiritual meat; And did all drink the same spiritual drink: for they drank of that spiritual Rock that followed them: and that ROCK WAS CHRIST* (emphasis mine).

Did you know that Jesus was back in the Book of Exodus? Those people drank from a spiritual Rock. Oh, but catch the next phrase — *the rock that followed them.* How in the world can a Rock follow you? Jesus was that Rock!

Jesus died on Calvary for your sins. He carried your sins. He carried my sins. But after He paid the price for our sins, He told the disciples to go to Jerusalem and wait for the promise of the Father. The Promise couldn't come until Jesus left and sent

Him to them. And those disciples received power after the Holy Ghost came on them.

You are Jesus' disciples today. That same power comes on you! Jesus said, "...out of your belly shall flow RIVERS OF LIVING WATER!" That's the water out of the Rock!

And if we can get this river flowing, that river will heal everything it comes in contact with. Do you believe that? *It will heal everything!*

Jesus said, *"The Spirit of the Lord is upon me..."* (see Luke 4:18). He never performed one miracle until He got the Holy Ghost. He never opened one blind eye, never unstopped a deaf ear, never made a lame man walk, until the Holy Ghost came on Him.

We Need the Holy Ghost

John the Baptist was baptizing in the Jordan when, all of a sudden, he saw Jesus coming down that dusty road. He stopped preaching, turned around, and said, "Behold, the Lamb of God that takes away the sins of the world! This is the One I've been waiting for. I've baptized you with water, but there is One that comes after me that shall baptize you with the Holy Ghost and with fire." (see John 1:29-33)

I know what you're going to say. You say your church doesn't believe in that. Believe it anyway. Believe it because the Bible says so. You don't have to follow the church. You don't have to follow men that don't believe in the Bible. Follow Jesus.

Jesus knew He needed the Holy Ghost so He had John baptize Him. He went down in the water and when He came up out of that water something happened. Somebody said a dove came on Him. Oh, no. It was the Holy Ghost in the form of a dove.

I say it was the dove that Noah sent flying out of the Ark looking for somebody to land on! It flew over Moses. It flew over Joshua. It flew over David. It flew over all the prophets. It did all that flying and its wings were getting kind of heavy. All of a sudden, it saw Jesus coming up out of the water, and that Dove said, "This is the One I was looking for." And the Dove of the Holy Ghost lighted right on Jesus.

After Jesus got the Holy Ghost, He went about doing good, healing all that were sick and oppressed of the devil. Jesus needed the Holy Ghost. And if He needed the Holy Ghost, you and I need the Holy Ghost. Baptists and Methodists, Presbyterians and Episcopalians, Pentecostals and Charismatics, we all need to be filled with the Holy Ghost! I'm asking God to give you a double portion of the Holy Ghost. I want to see you get a double portion of Him.

We're living in a double portion age. God is getting ready to use His people. The Church is coming alive, and we're going to put the devil where he belongs — under our feet.

God wants to lead you and me in everything that we do. And He'll do that by the Holy Spirit. He said when the Spirit of truth came that He would lead and guide you into all truth. So if you're telling me your church doesn't believe in this, you're letting me know the Holy Ghost isn't leading you.

You say, "My pastor doesn't believe in this."
Find a pastor that does.   This is Bible.
Everything the Holy Spirit will lead you into can be
found right here in the Word of God — the Spirit and
the Word will always agree.

Lean on the Rock

Now go back to Moses at the rock.   Do you
know how much water you need to quench the thirst of
three and a half million people?   That's a whole lot of
water.   The Bible says the water gushed out.   Not only
for the people, but for all their animals.   *And that rock
followed them.*

How can a rock follow?   The water, when it
came out, seeped down into the ground and formed an
underground pool.   And everywhere the cloud of the
Holy Ghost led the people, Jesus, the Rock, followed
them.

So whenever they got thirsty, all those women
got around with their timbrels and started to sing,
"Spring up, oh well."   And the men began to dig and
the water would come springing forth again —
symbolizing the Holy Ghost.

At times you and I are called to go through
seasons of dryness.   You may even start to wonder
whether or not there is a God.   Everything seems dry
and dead.   Then you get revived in your spirit and the
wells of water come springing up.   Before long, you
get your joy back and say, "Oh, Lord, I never did lose
it — it's just been going underground.   But thank God,

it's coming out in a geyser!"

That's the discipline of the thirsty place — learning to lean on the Rock called Jesus until the water of the Holy Ghost quenches your thirst.

But there was a second period in the history of these people when they got thirsty again. Moses struck that rock twice. Remember the story? And because he struck that rock twice, God told him he wasn't going into the Promised Land.

God wants you to be led of His Spirit. He may lead you to do one thing one way, but that doesn't mean for you to get in a rut and do it again the same way. Every time you move, get your orders from heavenly headquarters. I'm talking about God.

God only told Moses to strike the rock once. Oh, this sends chill bumps up and down my spine, folks.

Jesus Christ was only crucified *one* time. You can't crucify Him again. They put Him on a cross — *once*. He died but once, once and for all.

Speak to the Rock

You say, "But what if I get thirsty again?"

The children of Israel got thirsty again. And God said to Moses, "Don't strike that rock now, all you need to do is *talk* to the rock." Isn't that beautiful? *Speak* to the rock. All you have to do is talk to the rock and the water will come flowing out. Hallelujah! The Rock is Jesus. And you can speak to Him in prayer.

Whenever you need something from God, all you have to do is ask the Father in Jesus' name, and He'll give it to you. Beloved, that's where we are right now. Jesus said you have not because you ask not. The reason you don't have is because you don't ask. You take it for granted.

I'll never forget praying for a lady in our church in Philadelphia. She was on her knees in the corner, and she was moaning, "Oh, Jesus. Please, Jesus. Please, Jesus. Please, Jesus..."

I didn't embarrass her. I went over to where she was, knelt beside her, put my arm around her, and whispered in her ear, "Change one word, sweetheart. Change the 'please' to 'thank you.'"

You see, God's already made provision for whatever you ask of Him. So after you ask, don't keep begging. Begin thanking Him for the answer.

This dear lady did what I told her to do. She started saying, "Thank You, Jesus. Thank You, Jesus." She got up off her knees, dried her tears, started dancing, and said, "My God, I got it. Thank You, Jesus. Thank You, Jesus. Thank You, Jesus. I got it. It belongs to me. My God, I got it. It's mine!"

You're not a beggar. I'm not a beggar. We are the sons of God! We are heirs of God. We are joint-heirs with Jesus Christ. Everything that Jesus owns, Schambach's part owner of it. And if I'm part owner, you're part owner of all of Heaven's riches, too. Whatever you need from God, Jesus will supply.

I was holding a meeting in Peoria, Illinois. After I checked into my hotel, I got hungry and went down to get a turkey sandwich. I sat down in the restaurant and across from me sat five men around a table. I saw them look at me and start whispering to each other. I thought, *Oh, oh, they know me.*

One of them came over and asked if I was Brother Schambach. I said, "Yes."

He said, "We're all Baptist preachers, and we traveled 275 miles to hear you preach tonight. Can we join you?"

I said, "Let me join you. No use in five moving; let me move."

I spent three hours with them. It was the most delightful time I've ever spent with five men. Do you know what those Baptist preachers told me? They went to Southern University in Louisville, a Baptist university, to study for the ministry. They said, "You used to come on radio at a certain time." And every day they would all sneak out of class and get in their automobile just to hear me preach on the radio. One day I was preaching about the Holy Ghost and I dared all the Baptists to put their hands on the radio. (They were telling me all this.)

One of them said, "All five of us boys said, 'That Pentecostal preacher isn't going to dare us!' All five of us slapped our hands on the dash of the car. When we did, we landed on the floorboard, and came up talking in another language. We all got filled with the Holy Ghost!

"We heard you were going to be here so we wanted to come see you. We're pastoring Holy Ghost Baptist churches — healing the sick, casting out devils, and bringing deliverance to the people!" Hallelujah!

Aren't you glad He's still pouring out His Spirit?

You can drink of the Water of Life, Jesus, in the midst of the thirsty place, and never thirst again!

Chapter 6

The Place of Rest and Refreshing

And they came to Elim, where were twelve wells of water, and threescore and ten palm trees: and they encamped there by the waters (Exodus 15:27).

So far we have covered five areas of discipline. The first one is the discipline of the winding path. It will take you into areas where you never expected to be.

The second is the discipline of the impossible place. We always blame impossible situations on the devil. But sometimes God disciplines us in the impossible place so we can put our faith to work and watch God move. He turns the thing around and works it out for His glory.

Next is the discipline of the bitter place. You

may have had bitter experiences. But thank God, He has a way — the remedy is standing close by. No matter what situation you're in, when God gets done with it you're going to come out smelling like a rose.

Then there are the disciplines of the hungry place and the thirsty place.

Have you ever been hungry or thirsty? You say, "Why, Lord? Why do I have to suffer these indignities?" Just hang in there. God's not through yet.

You have wandered the winding paths. You've struggled with the impossible place. You've tasted the bitter places. You've searched for God in the hungry place, the dry place. But thank God for this one little verse of scripture in the 15th chapter of the Book of Exodus.

Right in the middle of all their wandering, God brought the Israelites to a place of refreshing. They stopped by 12 wells of water and 70 palm trees. It sounds like Palm Springs! Isn't that wonderful?

The time of rest and refreshing comes to the people of God after scenes of bitter trial. Weeping may endure for a night, but joy is going to come in the morning.

God has seen your tears. God has seen your trouble. He never left you. He was right there in the middle of that mess that you're in. But now He says it's time to get under a palm tree and rest. It's time to be refreshed.

God has a palm tree for every year of your life. He's got a well of spring water for every month of the year. The wells bring blessing and comfort. This is the place of refreshing where you can find rest for your weary soul.

Now look back at Exodus 15:9: *The enemy said, I will pursue, I will overtake, I will divide the spoil; my lust shall be satisfied upon them; I will draw my sword, my hand shall destroy them.*

Who is that talking? That's the devil — the same devil that held the Israelites in bondage and captivity.

Every believer who is saved and washed in the blood of the Lamb has been brought out of bondage and captivity by God. But there's a real world out there that is controlled by the devil — the thief that comes to steal, kill, and destroy. Thank God, Jesus came to give us life.

Now I would be content with that, but He didn't stop there. He said, *"...and that they might have it more abundantly"* (see John 10:10). It's time to rejoice. It's time to manifest the Spirit of God in such a way that we will have an abundant supply of everything that He has promised us!

You Can Be at Rest

We live in a restless world. People are living in anxiety. They are filled with fears, doubts, and unbelief. And not only the world's people, but church people are in the same boat. Fear, doubt, and unbelief prevail on every hand.

But God promised us peace. You'll never know what peace is outside of Jesus Christ. He is the only peace you can have. Read the 23rd Psalm in your devotional time. "The Lord is my Shepherd." He is the Shepherd of your soul and mine. He was the Good Shepherd then, but He is the Great Shepherd now.

The Good Shepherd laid down His life for the sheep. He did that 2,000 years ago. He was buried three days and three nights in the belly of this earth, and He came out of the grave victoriously. He ascended to Heaven and sat down at the right hand of God the Father. He became our *great* High Priest. He's sitting at the right hand of God, making sure you and I get everything promised to us in the Bible. He represents us before the Father. We represent Him down here in this world. Thank God, we can have perfect peace if our minds are stayed on Him.

Sure, we have storms in this life, but when the storm brews, you can still have peace. You can be at rest.

In Mark's Gospel, Chapter 4, Jesus was asleep in the hinder part of the ship on a pillow when the storm came. The disciples were fearful. They were filled with doubt. But Jesus was sound asleep. They were scared to death, but He was at rest.

You may have drug addicts on one side of you and alcoholics on the other. You may have gamblers behind you. But God can keep you in perfect peace right where you are because He is your peace.

People are scared to death about what the Russians are going to do to us. My God, they're not going to do anything to me. Sudden death, sudden glory! They can kill this body, but my life is hid with

Christ in God, and I have perfect peace with Him. Aren't you glad you are at rest with Jesus?

You Can Be Restored

Thank God for places of refreshing we can come to where the water is flowing like a river.

I want you to understand some things. First, water is a type of the Holy Ghost. The Israelites were around the twelve springs of water for a reason. I like to call them springs instead of wells. They were there for a time of refreshing, but also for a time of restoration. God is our Restorer.

When you came to Christ, you were a mess. Sin had taken its toll in your physical body. If you were hooked on drugs or alcohol, the effects of addiction made you an old man or old woman before your time. Isn't that true?

I'll never forget a certain lady in the church I used to pastor some years ago. After a service, she came to me and showed me a picture. My first reaction was, "Who is that ugly woman?" And I knew I'd said the wrong thing.

She said, "Brother Schambach, that's me. I just wanted you to see what I looked like while I was serving the devil."

"Now that God has saved you," I said smiling, "He's given you beauty for ashes. Look at you now, girl. God really did a work on you!" He had restored her beauty.

If you can find a picture of what you used to

look like before you got saved, you were a mess. Just look in the mirror now and see what God's done. He's restored all those years that you wasted out there in the world.

A Never-ending Source of Supply

Do you know what else the children of Israel found, encamped there by the waters? A place of supply.

How would you like to get into that place? Second Peter 1:3 says, God *hath given unto us all things that pertain unto life and godliness.* It already belongs to us. We are heirs of God, and joint-heirs with Christ.

I believe it's time we realize that every good and perfect gift comes from God. You may think you've acquired possessions and position because of your own abilities, wisdom, and knowledge. Not so! Just because you graduated from a university doesn't mean anything.

God is your Shepherd. He is the One who provides for you. He's the One who supplies every one of your needs according to His riches in glory by Christ Jesus.

We just don't realize who we are. We act like a bunch of paupers. We're God's people. We're sons and daughters of the King.

I was preaching in Chicago some years ago, and I got some great sermon material reading the newspaper. There was an enterprising reporter who went around visiting every banking institution in the city. He wanted to find out how much unclaimed money was in those banks, money left for an inheritance by someone who had died.

What he discovered would blow your mind. There was enough unclaimed money in the banks of Chicago alone to pay off the national debt! And he listed the names of people who had unclaimed money in two full-page ads for about 10 days.

I was there for a two-month revival and they hooked me for a newspaper every day. I didn't read the weather report. I didn't go to the sporting page. I went to the "name" page. I've been preaching in Chicago for 20 years. Maybe somebody died and put my name in a will!

I didn't look for the A's or the B's. I headed for the S's. I looked for Shamrock, Shucklebuck. I looked for Shadrach, Shambattle, Shambaugh, Shamshack — everything I've ever been called. One lady used to call me Brother Sandbox. So I looked for Sandbox. I was looking for any reasonable facsimile.

I bought a paper every day. But you can tell by looking at me, I didn't find my name. But I got a sermon out of it.

One man's name was listed, but he was so poor he couldn't even afford to buy a paper. He was on welfare. But his buddy saw his name on the list and came and told him, "Get dressed, man, you've got money in the bank. All you've got to do is go sign your name."

He said, "Not me. I never had nothing, and I never will. You ain't playing no game with me."

So the buddy got in touch with that reporter. He said, "Will you go with me? My friend won't believe me." The buddy introduced his friend to the reporter who wrote the story, even brought him the paper.

"Why," the man said, "there's more than one person with my name. I ain't never had nothing. I was born poor, I'm going to die poor. I ain't playing your game." They couldn't get him to go to the bank.

The reporter went to the editor. He got the editor to go out. The editor of the newspaper said, "It's your name, man. All you've got to do is sign your name."

But the man wasn't budging. "Nobody's playing no April fool's joke on me. I never had nothing, and never will."

Finally Mayor Daley heard about it. He said, "You mean to tell me, somebody's on welfare that has money in the bank!" He called his chauffeur. "Get the car ready. We're going to get him. We're not giving him any more city money as long as he's got money in the bank."

He drove out to see the man...didn't introduce himself...just knocked on the door and said, "Get in the car. We're going to get your money!"

To make a long story short, the man signed his name on the dotted line and became the recipient of $5 million. He paid back every dime he ever took on welfare. It turned out that a man he had befriended some 30 years earlier had died and put his name in the will. And he didn't even know it. That money had been in the bank for years, compounding interest day after day after day until it had multiplied to $5 million.

But I've got a better story to tell you. I know Somebody who died 2,000 years ago and left us His last will and testament. And it's been compounding interest for 2,000 years. I'm not talking about Rockefeller. I'm talking about JESUS.

And guess what? I found *your name* in the will. It doesn't matter where you've been or where you live, your name is in the will.

Where did I find your name? In Romans 8:14, *For as many as are led by the Spirit of God, they are the sons of God.* And if we are sons of God, we are heirs of God. And if we're heirs of God, we are joint-heirs with Jesus Christ — everything Jesus owns, we are part owner of (see vss. 15-17). This is your never-ending source of supply!

A lot of God's people have what I call the beggar's syndrome. Their prayers sound like this, "Please, Jesus. Please, Jesus. If it be Your will, Lord. Please..."

You're a child of God. All you have to do is say, "Thank You, Jesus. Thank You, Jesus. If You said it, You'll do it. If You spoke it, You'll bring it to pass. God cannot lie and I believe Your Word."

The Joy of the Lord Is Your Strength

You can also find the place of joy. Too many Christians look like they've been baptized in lemon juice! Jesus promised to give us joy that the world can't give and joy the world can't take from you. The joy of the Lord is your strength.

I get people in my prayer lines who say, "Pray that I'll get strength in the Lord." I'm not going to waste my prayers. Get some joy back — that's how you get strength! No wonder you're weak. Your joy has withered away.

You ought to go to church praising God. Enter into His courts with praise, into His gates with thanksgiving. Let everything that has breath, PRAISE THE LORD. I'm talking about joy, real joy.

The 23rd Psalm says, *my cup runneth over* (vs. 5). You get your cup running over and you'll splash it on your next door neighbor. They may look at you crosseyed for a while, but before long they are going to get with it.

No wonder the world won't get saved — they have to look at long, sad faces all the time. What in the world are we advertising anyway? When they see you so happy, they're going to say, what are you so happy about? Then you can share Jesus with them and get some more joy.

We were born to praise God. Aren't you glad you have joy? If you don't have it, the Bible says you can shout for it. I like to shout. The Church needs to do more shouting. I guarantee we'd have more joy!

If you want to learn how to praise the Lord, read the Psalms. David had a unique way of praising God. He praised the Lord in the morning, in the noontime, and when the sun went down. He made a habit of praise. Some of us only praise Him about once a month.

And ol' David got to feeling so good, he said,

"I'm going to have to write another psalm. Three times a day ain't enough. I'm going to praise Him seven times a day. I'm going to praise Him during my coffee break and on the way home. I'm going to praise Him at the supper table. And then I'm going to praise Him when I lay down and go to bed. And if I can't sleep at night, I'm going to get up and praise Him some more. I'm going to walk the floor and praise Him. Any way, any time, I'm going to praise the Lord. The joy of the Lord is my strength."

David got to praising God seven times a day and that wasn't enough. So he wrote another psalm and said, "His praise shall continually be in my mouth." If all we ever did for 24 hours a day was praise the Lord, we would really move God. He's waiting for praise.

I'll tell you how to get what you need from God. Try praising Him. Learn how to shout it out. The world has a product to get dirt out of your collar. They say, "*Shout* it out." It's about time we bring shouting back into the Church. Get rid of the arthritis. Get rid of the rheumatism. Get rid of the sickness. Get rid of the disease. Praise it out. Get some old-fashioned joy by praising God. The joy of the Lord is your strength!

OTHER MATERIALS BY

POWER PUBLICATIONS

Books

By R. W. Schambach

You're One In A Million
Power Over Temptation
How To Heal The Sick, Cast Out Devils And Still Go To Hell
Power for Victorious Christian Living
Four Lambs
Miracles: Eyewitness To The Miraculous
You Can't Beat God Givin'
What To Do When Trouble Comes
I Shall Not Want
The Secret Place
After The Fire
The Miracle Manual *An Evangelism and Prayer Handbook for the "One Million Souls" Campaign*
The Power Walk Diary

By Donna Schambach

Tell, Teach & Train

By A. A. Allen

God's Guarantee To Heal You
The Price Of God's Miracle Working Power
Demon Possession Today And How To Be Free

Videos

Fabulous Fakes *A Religion Of Form Vs. A Religion of Force*
Miracles
The Army Of The Lord
How To Raise The Dead
A Life Of Faith
Turn Up The Heat
Don't Touch That Dial
The Great Grave Robbery

Cassettes

Two Tape Series

Fabulous Fakes *A Religion Of Form Vs. A Religion of Force*
The Golden Scepter Of Deliverance
The Secret For Help
The Violent Take It By Force
Power Struggle
The Name Of Jesus
Making Jesus King
The Accomplishments Of Faith
After The Fire

Three Tape Series

A Chosen Generation (By Donna Schambach)

For more information about this ministry and a free catalog, please write:

SCHAMBACH REVIVALS, INC.
P. O. BOX 9009
TYLER, TX 75711-9009

To order materials by phone, call:

(903) 894-6131

WHEN YOU NEED PRAYER

Call the Power Phone

Every day of the week, 24 hours a day, a dedicated, faith-filled, Bible-believing Prayer Partner is ready to talk with you and pray about your needs. When you need prayer, call:

(903) 894-6141